A Bridge Through Grief

Grief

What do you do when your soul is thrust into the cold chaos of grief?

Joyce R. Jackson

Screven and Allen Publishing

ISBN-13: 978-1732292314 (Screven and Allen Publishing)
ISBN-10: 1732292314

Published by Screven and Allen Publishing

Cover Image: Pierre-August Renoir, La vague, 1879, provided by The National Gallery of Art, images.nga.gov

A significant quote was found after the body of this book was written. "Consciously recognizing the emotions reduced their impact." Alex Korb, Ph.D., The Upward Spiral, Using Neuroscience to Reverse the Course of Depression, One Small Change at a Time, Oakland, CA: New Harbinger Publications, Inc. 2015, page 44.

Dedication:

To David who dries my tears,

to Michael whose many lanterns light our family bridge,

and

to the One who binds up the broken hearted and breathes hope into the darkness, making it light.   *Psalm 147:3*

Introduction:

This is a field guide, designed to help the hurting find steady footing by building a bridge through grief that honors their loved one, the truth and the processing of events. There is a danger in putting events into writing that implies chronological processing. One who grieves is caught in a storm surge of afflictions that assault randomly and at times simultaneously. This field guide helps identify the landmarks that are a part of that process but a person may find themselves tossed about among the landmarks in random order. This chaos highlights the need of building a bridge through to keep from being lost in the storm.

The sketch pages are for personal notes, thoughts, images or ideas that reveal the specifics of the reader's own process. Such personal notes bring the pain into the light where it can be processed.

It is recommended that the hurting find a counselor, minister or trusted friend to be a support through this process. Leaning into strong relationships is a sign of a healthy person.

The Crossing:

Have you ever stepped into a stream so cold that it makes your head spin? The icy current curls around your toes as you search for solid rock beneath the surface to steady yourself. Resting on a solid foundation makes that experience secure. Finding sure footing on that stable stone helps you maneuver safely across.

While this guide will help you find firm footing it is important to start where you are. On the sketch page describe your current state. What disorienting forces are you experiencing?

Sudden Impact:

The storm of tragedy strikes unleashing a flash flood of details and emotion that seem to assault from every direction. Being overwhelmed is normal when normal has suddenly been obliterated. First reports of tragedy do not tell the whole story. Do not rush to judgment but propel yourself forward to do what you must do. Those who serve the grief stricken can be supportive or take advantage. Trusted friends who have weathered a similar storm well give the most honest guidance.

What are your top five concerns for the immediate future?

You are in the storm.

Cry
Pray
Breathe
Reach out

Don't be pressured into hasty decisions. Those who have experienced a similar tragedy will be your best allies. Who can you turn to and what do you need from them?

The Storm is in You

Suffocating pain and sorrow assault in waves. Thoughts swirl around you and sensations deeper than thoughts slice through you. Overwhelming emotion saturates your senses and oppresses every inch of your mind and body. During the ebb between the waves it is possible to process small bits of information.

Take time for your mind and body to respond to the trauma. Let the pain surface now or it will surface later in unhealthy ways. In what ways is the stress being translated into expression either intentionally or unintentionally?

Storm Surge

Anger is the fury of the storm but it isn't its substance. Capture each spur of anger, examine it as if it was a specimen in a jar. Discover the specific point of pain that each spur of anger emanates from. Say it aloud. "I am angry because…"

Anger is a current. It has energy and a source but the direction must be harnessed or it can cause great harm. Write it down as a means of exorcizing the anger. At each flame of fury say or write, "I am angry because…" This not only helps identify the specific issues that are surging through you but it helps differentiate the anger from you. Anger is something that you experience but you are separate from your anger. Search for the "why" of each pang of anger writing out each specific source.

Disaster Plan

Master anger or it will master you. It is time to build a disaster plan. What is the best action you can take for each spur of negative emotion? Or should you set this specific issue aside until you have more information? Share your thoughts and plans with someone whose perspective will give you an honest evaluation of your stance. Remember where you want to go is more critical than where you are. Let healthy goals drive your action plans.

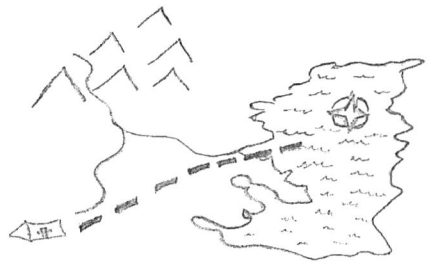

Search and Rescue

Sadness is pain that we wear like raindrops and floodwaters. It saturates so thoroughly that we feel one with it. Identifying the truth at the heart of each sadness pang can change it from a drowning flood into specific firm truths. As hard as those truths are this is how to find your footing. When the pain rises again, list each point specifically.

What is this pain emanating from?
Who is this truly focused on?
What is this pointing to?
What does it mean?

Searching out the truth will help you find honest footing to honor and respect the one you love.

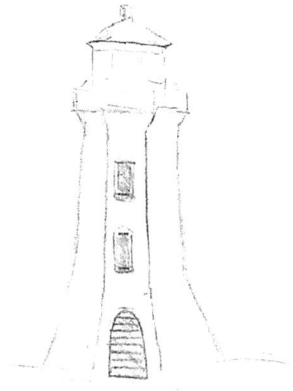

Building a Bridge

Identifying the specific causes of pain helps get a handle on the hard truths. Establishing truth will give you firm footing. Nail the hard truth of each specific pain down before you like planks on a bridge. Honesty is not disrespectful. Burying the truth is an obstruction to honoring the one you lost. Do not turn them into a two dimensional version or imagine them as someone different than who they truly were. Identifying the source of pain, start to lay down the hard truths before you. Those truths are solid footing for building a bridge through the fog of pain.

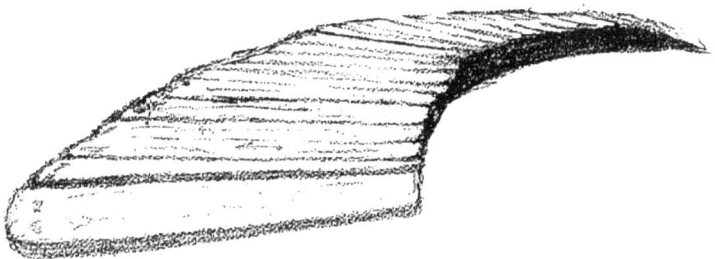

Points of Light

Search out and identify those points of light that you experienced together. Capture them in your mind. When was the last time their laughter rolled through the house? What was their favorite food, game or place? What special abilities did they have? What quirky habits did they have? What made them happy? Sad? Angry? Find the things that make you remember the best of your loved one. Be very specific. Share the details with others. Find photos, paint pictures in your mind. These will become great treasures but only if they're captured, remembered, shared. These memories become lights for you. Imagine a foot bridge through the storm illuminated by lanterns. Each positive memory is a lantern along the footbridge. Good memories when held high provide illumination for your path forward.

Renovation of the Soul

There is a tear in the fabric of your life, a hole in your heart. Instead of closing it up tightly, allow yourself to heal open and honest. Anger held in a tight grip is self poisoning. Beware the pit of despair. Sadness is a shroud that can both blind and bind. Acknowledge the loss and choose to live so that you honor this person in a positive way? What would they like to see you do? What would you want for them if they were in your place? What small steps can you choose to take in a positive direction?

Suddenly Adrift

Even after taking all the right steps and remembering all the right precious moments there are times when a rogue wave of grief will sweep you right back into the deep. You will find that you're suddenly adrift again. As with a rip current, do not focus on the pull. Focus on the stable high ground. Instead of fighting the current, take time to acknowledge it. Then move towards the firm foundation of truth and the illuminating light of good memories to cross the tide to find safe ground.

Grief comes in waves.
　　Grief comes of its own accord.
　　　Grief has no timetable or expiration date.
　　　Grief is love turned inside out.

No one is an Island

To keep firm footing on safe ground you need companionship. While it is true that no one can feel the exact grief that you feel, you need connection and understanding from others. Sharing your pain requires humility. And humbly admitting that you are human and hurting puts you on the path to healing. Those who do not let others in do not heal. The pain ices over and finds new avenues of outlet. Allowing your pain to be expressed to others lets the pressure release so you can find healing. The loss never leaves, but you can choose to hold onto the pain and move away from life or to release the pain by telling others and move towards life. Who can you open up to?

A Break in the Storm

There is more room to love in a broken heart. Even while your own heart is aching you will gain new capacity for compassion. You understand sorrow. You have the ability to lift others up. Ask yourself, "What can I say to encourage them? How can I help them find their way? What can help them see their next step?

In repurposing your grief experience to help others, you are better able to separate the person that you love from the pain of losing them. You are more free to remember them fully because the loss experience is separate from who they are.

In sharing what you know you are tossing a grieving person a life preserver. Still, you cannot force a person to grasp the life preserver. Offer what you have but let the professionals carry the heavy weight. Just as a drowning victim may bring others down in their state of panic those who are grieving may attempt to place too much on your shoulders. Share the food from your own plate of experience but know that they will also need support from other sources.

The Open Door

You have been swept away and found your footing again. You have built a bridge forward by establishing the solid foundation of truth, hard as it may be. You have built upon that by identifying your anger and deciding whether and what should be done with each spur. You have given grief its opportunity to examine each facet of your loss. You have placed lanterns of good memories to light your bridge by capturing those moments and lifting up the best of your loved one for everyone to see. You have chosen to grieve with an open heart to experience and express the pain without letting the pain drown out your identity or the love you have. You know that rogue waves will pound and currents will threaten to pull you under but you also know to open the door to friends and find refuge from the storm until you can see the *terra firma* of truth once again. The truth, the whole truth is that love always out shines and out lasts the storm.

Addendum:

Questions to identify anger or sadness:
Instead of being swept along by a giant storm of grief take a breath and in the midst of the pain pause to sort out who or what is the focus of this specific moment. The pain is real and spurred by some specific thought. Capture that spur. Name it. Know that this specific wound is the reality that your mind, heart and body are engaged in grappling with this fact.

Are you sad because of:
What this person suffered –
What this personal is missing out on –
Promises they can no longer keep -
Promises you can no longer keep -
Challenges you have to face alone –
The affect this has on others -
What you will miss –
Opportunities lost –
What your loved ones lost –
What should have been –
Missing their presence –
Disappointment -
Hope lost –
Fear –
Extinguished dreams –
Abandonment –
Loneliness –

Identifying specific points of pain helps to place those realities like memorial stepping stones through the grief. Naming them, knowing them turns the raging wind and driving rain into solid truths. Finding footing on these solid truths allows the storm to be real and honest without being lost within it.

Quick Lessons for Comforters:

1. The Power of Presence: There is no substitute for being there. Physical touch is powerful. It both gives strength and removes burdens. Skin on skin touch (provided it is appropriate for the closeness of the relationship) accomplishes what no words or pictures can capture.

2. The Power of Voice: Saying something is better than saying nothing. Saying too much can be worse than saying nothing as the words become unintended weapons. Remember this isn't about you. Mention your own trials if you have experienced the same situation since it does help the grieving to know that they are not alone in their experience. But do not use this as an opportunity to address your own pain as the grieving have enough to bear.

3. The Power of Anger: Psychology basics teach that anger is the result of blocked expectations. Death and disaster are the ultimate experience in blocked expectations. Expect anger to surface. Plans, hopes, even normal life activities that one depended on continuing are dashed. Anger isn't wrong but it may be wrongly placed or wrongly held to rather than moving through it to a healthier place. Trying to talk a grieving person out of their anger is as effective as fighting the wind. Much better to use the wind or anger to move you forward than to stand in its way shaking in its force.

Anger may also be a way of hanging on, not letting go. As long as one is angry, they are still locked in the situation, still engaged even if it makes them miserable. Anger is a power move, but in this case the effort is moot as the anger will not change the situation.

Anger is a normal, even necessary part of the process because it helps address reality. Defining anger specifically is an important step to finding how to turn anger into a tool for refining understanding. Upon examination in may be that anger is forcing the grieving to find a new perspective and path forward. Anger may also be an unrealistic covering for anguish or a deflection from fear, pain or hopelessness.

To seek truth, ask yourself what the real focus of your anger is? Anger needs to be moved through before grief can process. Anger is unresolved business. It is easier to remain angry and than to face grief. Identifying the core of what is fueling your anger. By naming the anger triggers or sources, they can be seen apart from self. Then for each anger source decide the best action to take. In doing so the situation is directed into healthy action instead of letting anger run life.

4. Ultimate comfort: Everyone leans on some standard as their basic source of truth. Without that foundation there is no way to build an understanding of reality or how the world functions. Recognizing that each person is responsible for identifying truth for themselves, I make no apologies for leaning on the Truth that guides me. This Truth is my lighthouse and my lifeboat. This Truth is my hope in the storm.

Creator God made all that is including you. The intricacy, power and orchestration of the universe points to His wisdom, strength and goodness. He knows and loves you as a caring father.

The first people of God's creation chose against him and breaking their intimate relationship with God and each other. They also brought brokenness to all of creation. All suffering, greed, sickness, pain, sorrow and death result from this brokenness. We suffer from this brokenness and continue in the path of our ancestors by choosing to act selfishly. God sent his perfect son, Jesus, to live as an example and to sacrifice His life to pay the price for each person's selfishness and brokenness. We can accept that payment to free us by admitting our selfish thoughts and actions and acknowledging Jesus as the one true God and king of our life.

Those who do choose to follow Jesus have eternal life for their soul and will live in peace for eternity with a loving God. Those who reject God are stuck in brokenness and will one day enter into an eternity without peace, forgiveness and truth.

I do not choose to believe this because it is comfortable but because it is true. I do not blame God for suffering any more then I blame a firefighter for a house fire. Jesus lived and died to rescue those willing to follow Him. One day all evil and suffering will be put to an end. But putting an end to suffering will mean putting an end to earth as we know it, halting all chances for souls to choose Him. Holy God is waiting to give another person a chance to choose life in Him.

Knowing that the ones I love walk with God daily and will have a good eternity with Him is the ultimate comfort during times of grief. For those who have not chosen to follow God by accepting the forgiveness and reconciliation offered by Jesus as long, as you have breath you have an opportunity to find this peace.

Resources:

While the author did not quote information from these sources directly, these sources have been so heavily relied upon over time that their wisdom is unalterably entwined with the author's own thoughts and writings.

Holy Bible: John, Chapter 3
Larry Crabb Jr, Ph.D, *The PaPa Prayer, The Prayer You've Never Prayed*, Nashville: Thomas Nelson, 2006
Focus on the Family: Radio programing and counseling services
Mark Batterson, *The Circle Maker, Praying Circles Around Your Biggest Dreams and Greatest Fears*, Grand Rapids: Zondervan, 2016
Mark Buchanan, *The Holy Wild, Trusting in the Character of God*, Grand Rapids: Multinoma Books, 2003
Henry Cloud Ph.D and John Townsend Ph.D., *Boundaries, When to Say Yes, When to Say No to Take Control of Your Life,* Grand Rapids: Zondervan, 2004

www.ingramcontent.com/pod-product-compliance
Lightning Source LLC
Chambersburg PA
CBHW071751020426
42331CB00008B/2276